Donated by:
Target Stores

For Carlyn and Maren, my little mermaids,
and Tate, my sailor buoy —K. W. K.

To my father-in-law, Bing Mah:
Thanks for all the help and support
over the years —N. W.

Henry Holt and Company, LLC
Publishers since 1866
115 West 18th Street
New York, New York 10011
www.henryholt.com

Henry Holt is a registered trademark of Henry Holt and Company, LLC
Text copyright © 2003 by Kathleen W. Kranking
Photographs copyright © 2003 by Norbert Wu
Distributed in Canada by H. B. Fenn and Company Ltd.

Library of Congress Cataloging-in-Publication Data
Kranking, Kathy. The ocean is . . . / Kathleen W. Kranking ; photographs by Norbert Wu.
Summary: The reader is invited on an underwater tour of the ocean to view the varied
plant and animal life there. [1. Ocean—Fiction. 2. Marine biology—Fiction.
3. Marine plants—Fiction. 4. Stories in rhyme.] I. Wu, Norbert, ill. II. Title.
PZ8.3.K8635 Oc 2003   [E]—dc21   2002004594
ISBN 0-8050-7097-4 / First Edition—2003 / Designed by Donna Mark
Printed in the United States of America on acid-free paper. ∞
10 9 8 7 6 5 4 3 2 1

The photos in this book show: (title page) green sea turtles; (8–9) California sea lions; (10–11) soft coral,
fairy basslets; (12–13) main: bigscale soldierfish, bluestripe snapper; inset: Caesar grunts; (14–15) elephant
ear sponge, black-tipped fusiliers; (16–17) bottlenose dolphins; (18–19) main: sea urchins, starfish; inset:
candy cane starfish; (20–21) sea otter; (22–23) whitetip reef shark, goby; (24–25) main: clinging crab,
sea fan; inset: longnose hawkfish, sea fan; (26–27) giant kelp; (28–29) humpback whale.

The Ocean Is...

Kathleen W. Kranking

photographs by

Norbert Wu

Henry Holt and Company

New York

Salt and surf and sand and waves,
The ocean's these and more.
Come see what else! Dive in and take
An underwater tour.

The ocean is . . .
A PLAYGROUND

Seaweed for hide-and-seek,
Fish to chase, rocks to climb.
Sea lions have it made:
It's recess all the time!

The ocean is . . .
A GARDEN

Corals bloom beneath the waves,
Just like a garden grows.
But if you try to sniff *these* blooms,
There's water up your nose!

The ocean is . . .
 A TRAFFIC JAM

Fin to fin and nose to tail,
Together all the while.
Speeding up, then slowing down,
It's rush hour—fishy style!

The ocean is . . .
AN ART MUSEUM

Artists must work night and day
To make a sculpture look just so.
This sponge makes art the easy way:
All it has to do is grow.

The ocean is . . .

A STAGE

These dolphins dance and leap above
Their watery arena,
Performing like a graceful pair
Of long-nosed ballerinas.

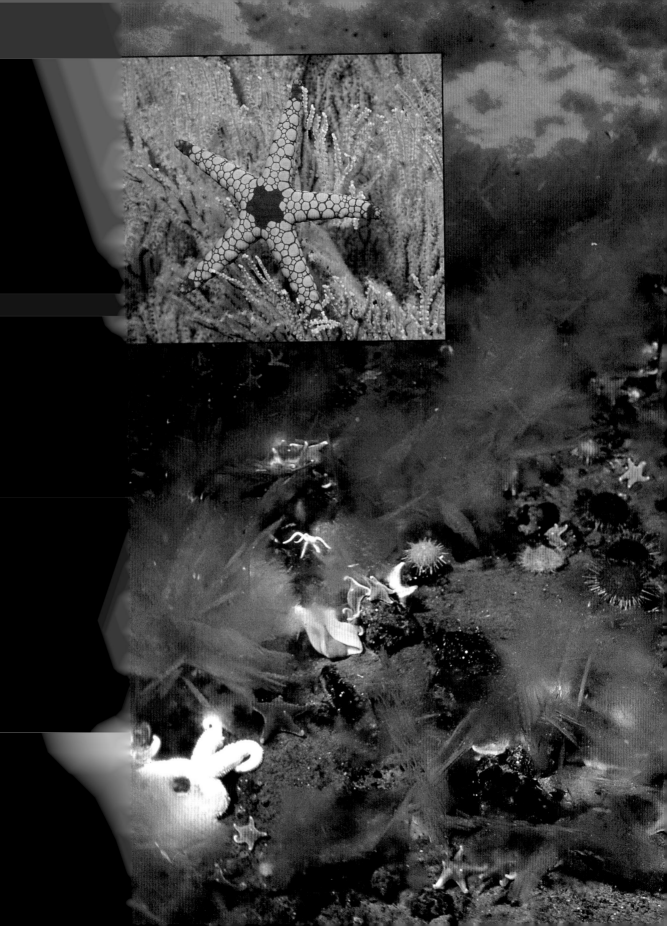

The ocean is . . .
A GALAXY

When you wish upon a star,
Don't look up at the sky,
For the brightest stars around
Aren't always high and dry.

The ocean is . . .
A CAFETERIA

There's shellfish on the menu,
An otter's favorite lunch.
Floating in the deep blue sea,
What better way to munch?

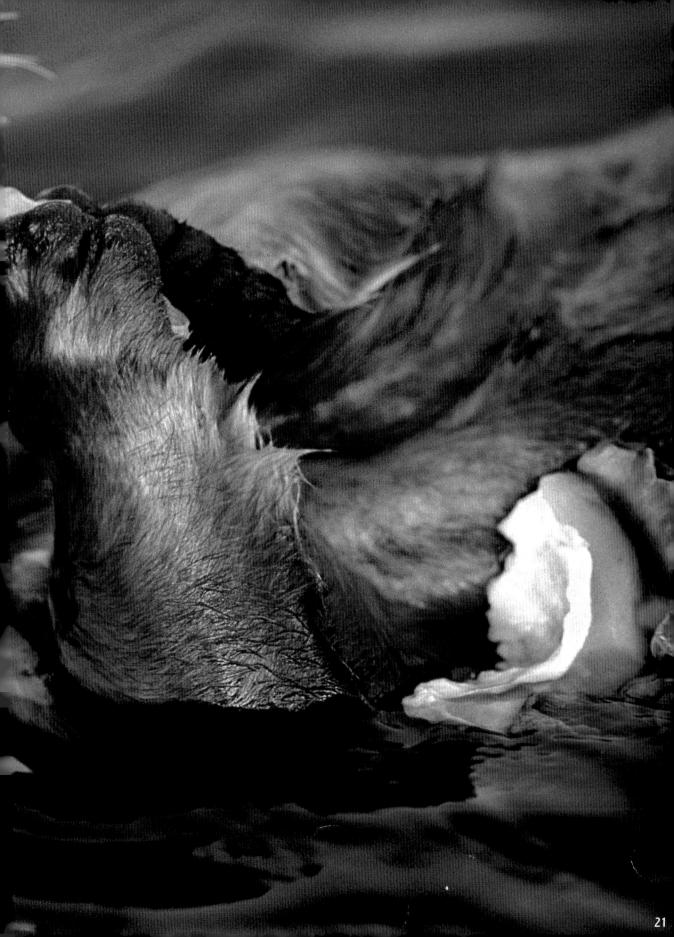

The ocean is . . .
A DENTIST'S OFFICE

A tiny dentist waits
For this shark to open wide.
To clean between those pointy teeth,
It bravely swims inside.

The ocean is . . .

A SECRET HIDEOUT

To fool our hungry enemies,
Who'd eat us in one bite,
We do a disappearing act
By hiding in plain sight.

The ocean is . . .
A FOREST

Here's something kind of fishy—
A forest in the sea!
Towering beneath the waves
Are swaying seaweed trees.

So now you know the ocean is
Much more than meets the eye.
The time has come to say so long.
You'd better go get dry!

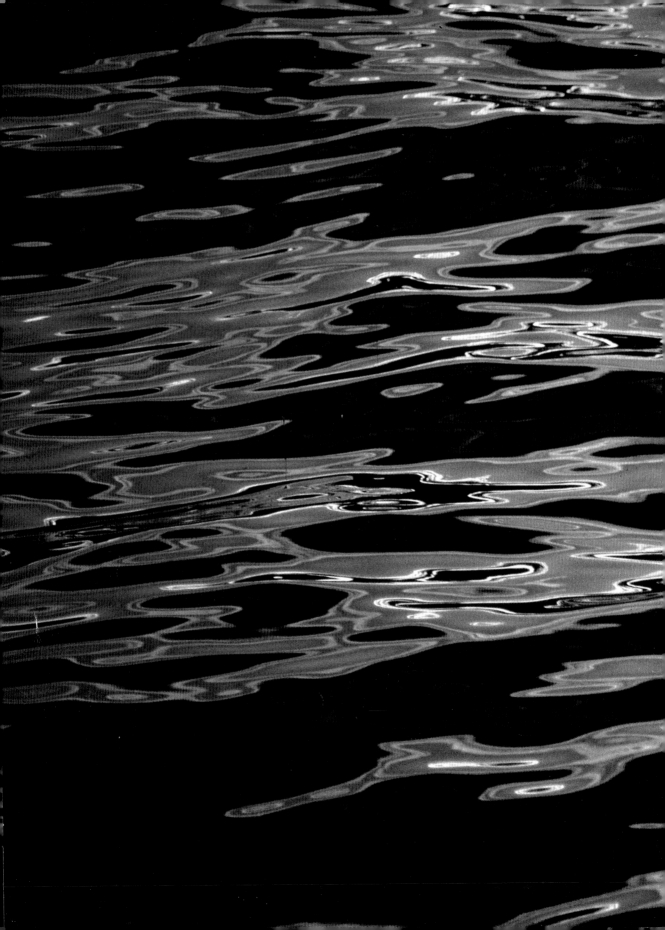